NATIONAL GEOGRAPHIC

Floods

EXTREME WEATHER

Josie Green

PICTURE CREDITS

page 1 © AFP/Corbis; page 4 (bottom left) Despotovic Dusko/Corbis Sygma; page 5 (top) © Getty Images; page 6 © Paul A. Souders/Corbis; page 9 (left) © Carl & Ann Purcell/Corbis; page 10 © Najlah Feanny/Corbis Saba; page 13 (top) © Stock Image Group/SPL; page 13 (bottom) © Tom Bean/Corbis; page 15 © Stock Image Group/SPL; page 16 © AFP/Corbis; page 21, 24 © ONF/Gamma; page 25 Shehzad Noorani-Still Pictures/Auscape; page 26 © AFP/Mufty Munir.

Produced through the worldwide resources of the National Geographic Society, John M. Fahey, Jr., President and Chief Executive Officer; Gilbert M. Grosvenor, Chairman of the Board; Nina D. Hoffman, Executive Vice President and President, Books and Education Publishing Group.

PREPARED BY NATIONAL GEOGRAPHIC SCHOOL PUBLISHING
Ericka Markman, Senior Vice President and President, Children's Books and Education Publishing Group; Steve Mico, Vice President and Editorial Director; Marianne Hiland, Executive Editor; Richard Easby, Editorial Manager; Jim Hiscott, Design Manager; Kristin Hanneman, Illustrations Manager; Matt Wascavage, Manager of Publishing Services; Sean Philpotts, Production Manager.

EDITORIAL MANAGEMENT
Morrison BookWorks, LLC

PROGRAM CONSULTANTS
Dr. Shirley V. Dickson, Program Director, Literacy, Education Commission of the States; James A. Shymansky, E. Desmond Lee Professor of Science Education, University of Missouri-St. Louis.

National Geographic Theme Sets program developed by Macmillan Science and Education Australia Pty Limited.

Published by the National Geographic Society
1145 17th Street, N.W.
Washington, D.C. 20036-4688

ISBN: 978-0-7922-4723-4
ISBN: 0-7922-4723-X

Product 4P41963

Printed in China by The Central Printing (Hong Kong) Ltd.
Quarry Bay, Hong Kong
Supplier Code: OCP May 2018
Macmillan Job: 804263
Cengage US PO: 15308030

MEA10_May18_S

Contents

Extreme Weather

The weather affects people's lives in many different ways. Weather helps people decide what clothes to wear, or what to do in their spare time. However, the weather can also be a matter of life and death. Extreme weather can be very severe. Droughts, floods, tornadoes, and hurricanes are all examples of extreme weather.

Key Concepts

1. **Conditions in the atmosphere, such as air pressure, create weather.**
2. **Clouds give meteorologists clues about what is happening in the atmosphere.**
3. **Tools and technology help meteorologists gather data about weather.**

Four Kinds of Extreme Weather

Droughts

Droughts happen when there is a lack of rain.

Floods

Floods happen when too much water flows over the land.

In this book you will learn about the causes and effects of floods like this one.

Tornadoes

Tornadoes are spinning wind funnels that create strong suction.

Hurricanes

Hurricanes are powerful storms with strong winds and heavy rains.

Weather and Floods

People often complain about wet weather. But most of the time, wet weather is good for people and the land. Rain supplies us with fresh water. It helps crops and other plants grow. However, too much rain can cause a lot of damage. When it rains heavily for days, the land cannot hold all the water. This can lead to **floods**.

Too Much Water

Floods happen when there is so much water on the land that the water cannot all drain away fast enough. The water pours into rivers. The rivers rise. The high water flows over the riverbanks and onto the land.

People wading through floodwater

Floodwaters can wipe out crops and destroy buildings. People and animals can drown. Diseases may be spread by the dirty floodwater.

It can take a long time for places to recover from a flood. People can be left without homes and food. It can take a long time for help to arrive if roads and bridges have been washed away by the flood.

Floods happen all over the world. But the worst floods happen where the land is flat and near sea level. The land floods easily when there are heavy rains.

Floods can block roads.

Places Where Floods Often Occur

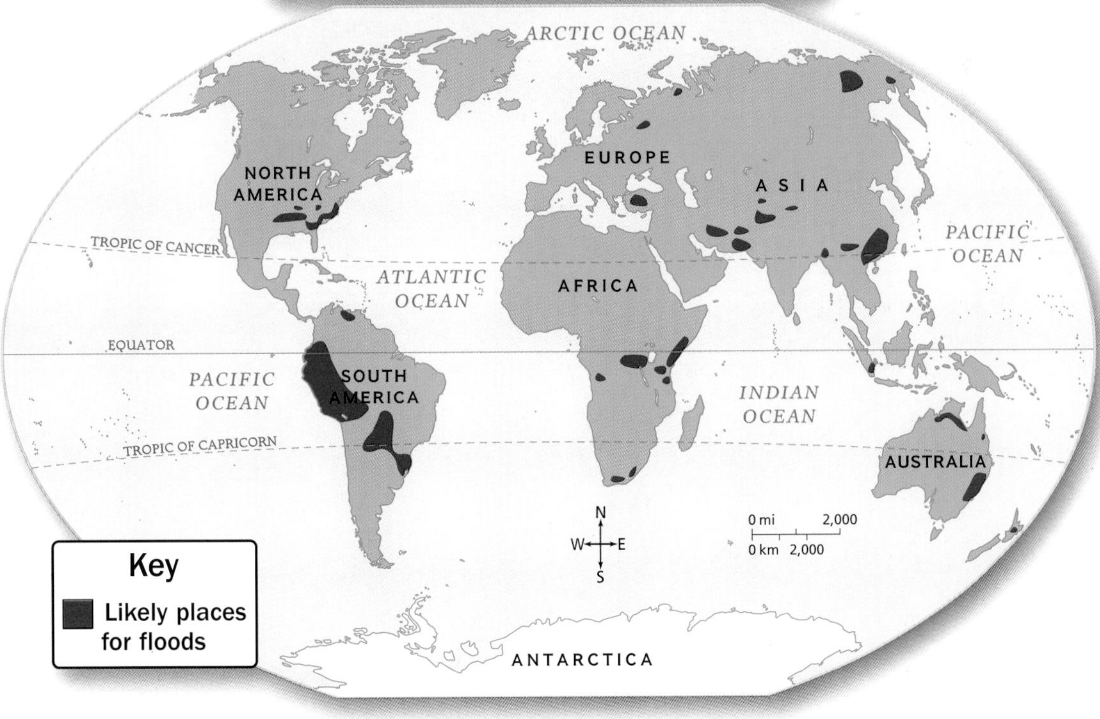

Key Concept 1 Conditions in the atmosphere, such as air pressure, create weather.

Where Rain Comes From

atmosphere
the layer of air that surrounds Earth

To understand what causes floods, you first need to understand how rain is formed. Rain comes from water in oceans, rivers, and lakes. When the sun warms the water, some of it turns into **vapor**. Vapor is very tiny drops of water in the air. The vapor rises into the **atmosphere**, the layer of air that surrounds Earth.

As the vapor rises higher, it cools down and turns into bigger drops of water. These drops of water form clouds. As the air gets colder, the drops get bigger and heavier until they fall as rain.

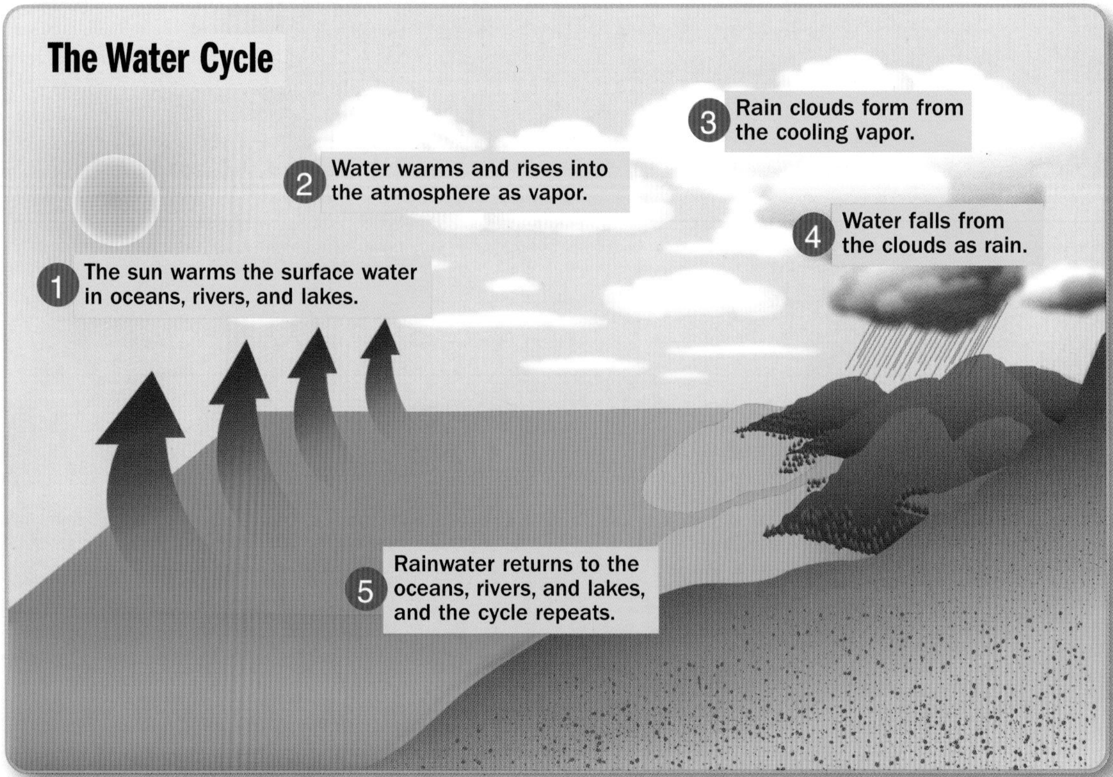

Air Pressure

Whether water vapor rises high enough to form rain clouds depends on air pressure. **Air pressure** is the air in the atmosphere pressing down on Earth.

air pressure
the effect of air pressing down on Earth's surface

When air is warmed by the sun, it becomes lighter and rises. The rising air reduces the amount of air pressure on Earth. This is called **low air pressure**. The rising air lifts water vapor into the air. The water vapor forms rain clouds.

When air above Earth cools, it becomes heavier and sinks. This heavy air creates **high air pressure** on Earth. High air pressure stops water vapor from rising and forming rain clouds, so it usually does not rain.

Wet weather is usually caused by low air pressure.

Clear weather is usually caused by high air pressure.

Why Floods Occur

Most floods occur when there is a lot of heavy rain. But rain isn't the only cause of floods. Hurricanes and melting snow can also cause serious floods.

Too Much Rain

Too much rain is the cause of most floods. Low air pressure and a weather condition known as a **front** usually bring rain.

Fronts occur when an area of warm moist air and an area of cold air meet. The warm air rises over the cold air. As it rises, the warm air cools and forms rain clouds. A front can bring heavy rain. If there is too much rain for the rivers to carry away, the rivers will overflow and flood the surrounding land.

A car is almost covered by floodwaters in North Dakota, 1997.

Hurricanes

Some floods are caused by **hurricanes**. Hurricanes are storms that start over warm seawater. These powerful storms are caused by warm, moist air rising from the ocean. As a hurricane gets close to land, strong winds can create huge waves. These huge waves can rush onto the land and cause serious floods. Hurricanes bring heavy rain, which increases the risk of flooding.

Hurricanes can create giant flood-causing waves.

Melting Snow

Floods can also be caused by melting snow. These floods occur if there is a lot of snow in the winter and the weather is warmer than usual in the spring. The warm weather may cause the snow to melt into water at a fast rate. If the ground and rivers cannot hold the water, there can be a flood.

Sometimes people can prepare themselves for flood conditions. If the weather is warmer than usual in the spring, people will know this may result in a flood.

Key Concept 2 **Clouds give meteorologists clues about what is happening in the atmosphere.**

Looking at Clouds

meteorologists scientists who study the weather

Meteorologists are people who study weather. One way meteorologists can predict the weather is by looking at clouds. There are many different types of clouds. Each type of cloud gives a clue about the weather to come. Cumulus, cumulonimbus, and nimbostratus clouds show that wet weather might be on the way. Too much rain can cause floods.

Cumulus Clouds

Cumulus clouds are puffy clouds. They look like cotton balls. These clouds do not usually bring rain themselves. However, they can grow into storm clouds. A towering cumulus cloud is a clue that a storm cloud might form. This cloud looks like a huge cauliflower. It has a flat base and a lumpy top. It can grow into a giant cumulonimbus.

Cumulus clouds look like giant cotton balls in the sky.

Cumulonimbus Clouds

Cumulonimbus clouds are large puffy clouds. They produce thunderstorms. Cumulonimbus clouds are the tallest of all clouds. They can be as tall as 18,300 meters (60,000 feet). They look like big towers in the sky. Heavy rain from cumulonimbus clouds can quickly flood an area.

Cumulonimbus clouds are towering storm clouds.

Nimbostratus Clouds

Nimbostratus clouds are thick, dark clouds that cover the sky and block out the sun. These clouds bring steady, often heavy, rain that can last for days. If the rain from these clouds is heavy enough or lasts long enough, it can cause flooding.

Nimbostratus clouds can bring heavy rain.

Key Concept 3 **Tools and technology help meteorologists gather data about weather.**

Predicting Floods

Meteorologists can predict, or **forecast**, floods by studying weather conditions. They use special tools to collect **data**, or information, on the weather. Computers turn the data into weather maps. Meteorologists look at the weather maps. They study information they have collected about floods in the past. They use all this information to predict when and where floods may occur. Rain gauges, radar, weather satellites, and flood-plain maps all help meteorologists forecast floods.

Predicted-Rainfall Map of the United States for September 1, 2003

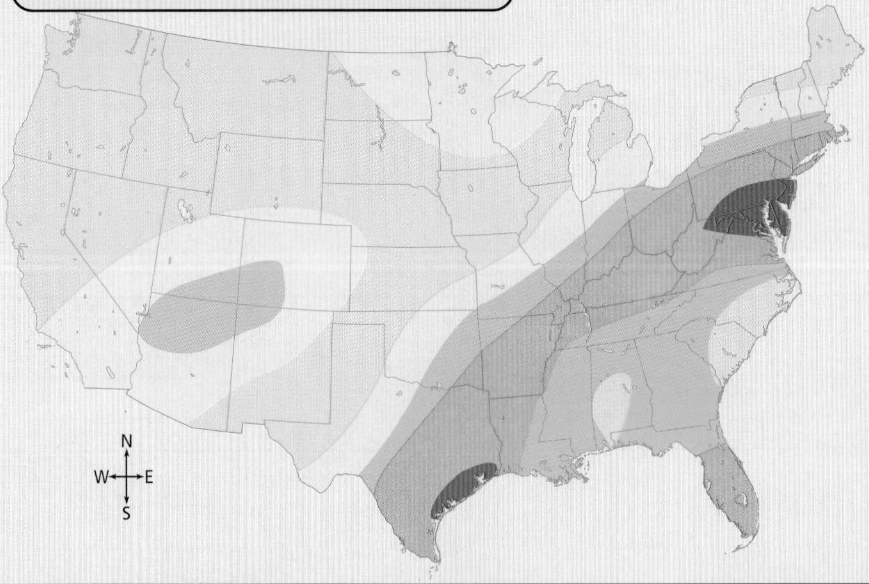

Key Predicted Rainfall: centimeters (inches)

0 | trace | 1 (.4) | 5 (2) | 10+ (4+)

Which region of the United States can expect the most rain, the Northeast or the Southwest?

Rain Gauges

A rain gauge measures how much rain a place receives. This tool is set in the ground. Rainwater collects in a tube with measurements marked on the side in millimeters or inches. The height of the water in the tube tells the meteorologist the amount of rain that has fallen. Rain gauges are useful tools. But they only show the rain levels in certain places. They do not give a full picture of rainfall.

A meteorologist checks a rain gauge.

Radar

Radar is another tool used to predict the amount of rainfall. An antenna on the radar scanner sends radio waves into the atmosphere. The radio waves reflect off raindrops and travel back to the antenna. The more waves that bounce back to the antenna, the heavier the rain. Meteorologists study the data from rain gauges and radar over time. They can then look for patterns. They can tell where and at which time of year a flood is most likely to occur.

Weather Satellites

Weather **satellites** travel around Earth. They take photographs of clouds. They send the photographs to weather offices. Meteorologists can tell from the photographs what kinds of clouds are forming. They can then predict if heavy rain or a hurricane that may cause flooding is likely to happen.

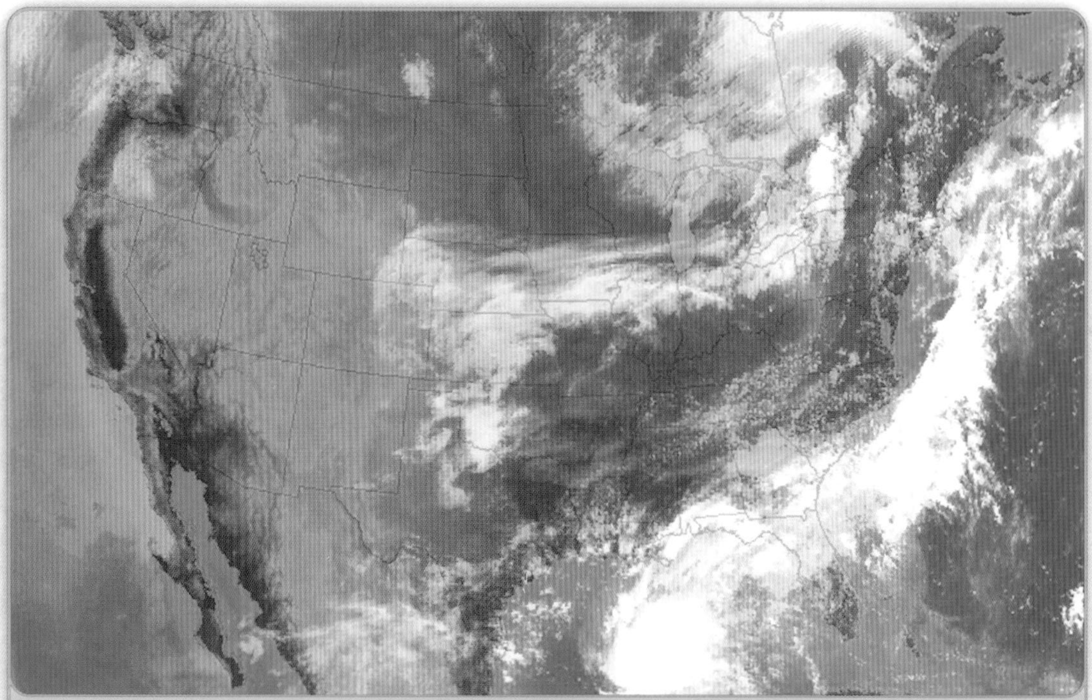

Weather satellite photographs showing cloud formations help meteorologists predict the weather.

Flood-Plain Maps

Flood plains are low-lying areas around rivers, lakes, and streams. They become flooded after heavy rains. Maps of flood plains are made from the records of past floods. Flood-plain maps can be used to predict which areas may flood again. They tell meteorologists how far a flood is likely to spread. These maps can also be used to let people know where it isn't safe to build their homes.

Think About the Key Concepts

Think about what you read. Think about the pictures and diagrams. Use these to answer the questions. Share what you think with others.

1. Name one kind of extreme weather. What conditions lead to this weather?

2. What can meteorologists learn about the weather from studying clouds?

3. What tools do meteorologists use to forecast the weather?

4. How does extreme weather affect people and the land?

VISUAL LITERACY

Weather Maps

Weather maps contain information that helps you understand the weather.

Look back at the weather map on page 14. It is a weather map of the United States. The map shows which places were expecting rain on a certain day.

The weather map on page 19 is a different kind of weather map. It shows weather conditions that will cause rainy weather in southeast Australia. To read a weather map, follow the steps below.

How to Read a Weather Map

1. **Read the title to learn what the map shows.**
   What is this weather map about?
2. **Read the key to learn what the symbols stand for.**
   What do the lines show? What do the letters L and H stand for?
3. **Study the information on the map.**
   Which city is likely to be having rainy weather? Why do you think that?
4. **Think about what you have learned.**
   If clear weather was likely in a city, would you expect to see a letter H or a letter L near that city on the map?

Rain Conditions in Australia

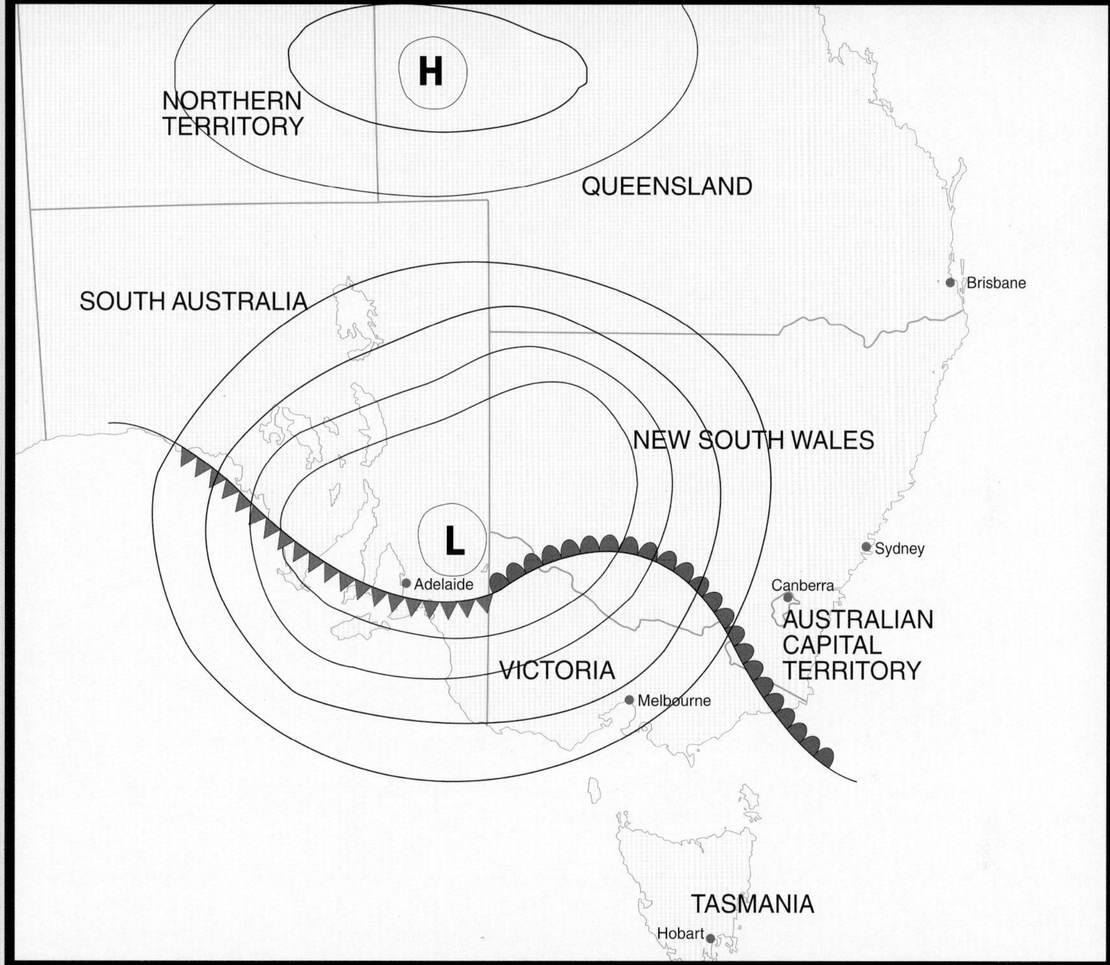

Key

L Area of low air pressure

H Area of high air pressure

Warm front – warm air meets and rises above cold air

Cold front – cold air meets and is pushed under warm air

Isobars – join areas that have the same air pressure

GENRE STUDY

Explanations

An **explanation** can tell how and why something happened. The article starting on page 21 tells about one specific weather event. It explains what happened, why it happened, and what effects it had on the people and land.

An explanation includes the following:

The Introduction
The introduction gives the reader an overview, or the big picture of what the explanation is about.

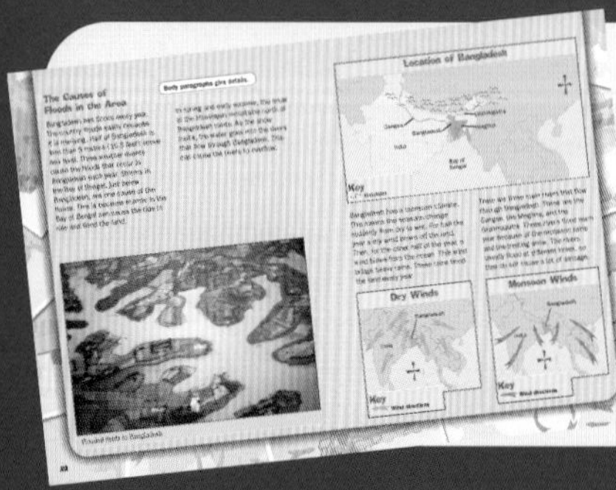

Body Paragraphs
The body paragraphs make up most of the writing in the explanation. They provide the information and details that help to explain the event.

The Conclusion
The conclusion summarizes or ties together the information in the explanation.

The Bangladesh Flood of 1998

The **title** tells you the topic.

Floods occur when it rains heavily and the land cannot hold all the water. In the summer of 1998, Bangladesh was hit by the worst flood of the twentieth century. Floodwater covered two thirds of the country.

The **introduction** tells you what the explanation will be about.

The flood affected more than 30 million people. Millions of people lost their homes and animals in the flood. Millions of people lost their land and livelihoods. However, the worst effect of the flood was that many people lost their lives.

Maps, diagrams, charts, and **photographs** help you picture what you are reading.

Medical help is given to sick and injured people during the 1998 flood.

The Causes of Floods in the Area

Body paragraphs give details.

Bangladesh has floods every year. The country floods easily because it is low-lying. Half of Bangladesh is less than 5 meters (16.5 feet) above sea level. Three weather events cause the floods that occur in Bangladesh each year. Storms in the Bay of Bengal, just below Bangladesh, are one cause of the floods. This is because storms in the Bay of Bengal can cause the tide to rise and flood the land.

In spring and early summer, the snow in the Himalayan mountains north of Bangladesh melts. As the snow melts, the water goes into the rivers that flow through Bangladesh. This can cause the rivers to overflow.

Flooded fields in Bangladesh

Location of Bangladesh

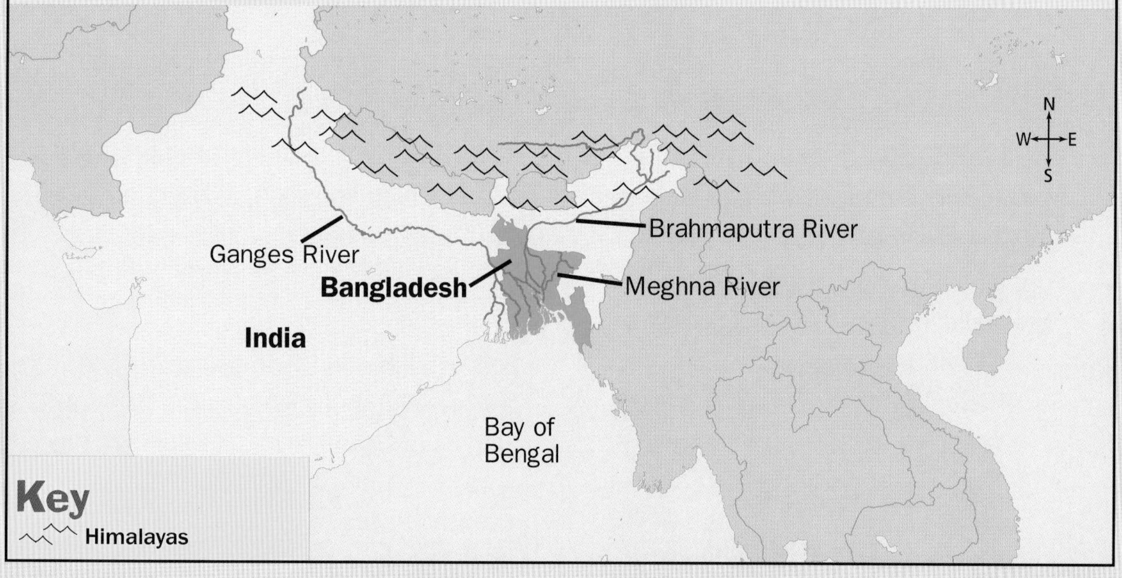

Bangladesh has a monsoon climate. This means the seasons change suddenly from dry to wet. For half of the year a dry wind blows off the land. Then, for the other half of the year, a wind blows from the ocean. This wind brings heavy rains. These rains flood the land every year.

There are three main rivers that flow through Bangladesh. These are the Ganges, the Meghna, and the Brahmaputra. These rivers flood each year because of the monsoon rains and the melting snow. The rivers usually flood at different times, so they do not cause a lot of damage.

Dry Winds

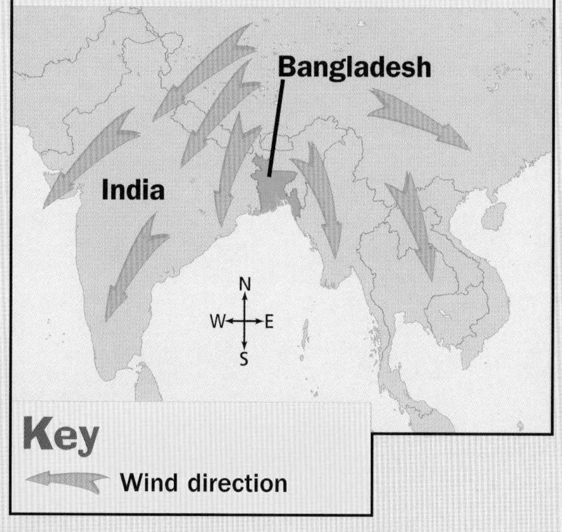

Monsoon Winds

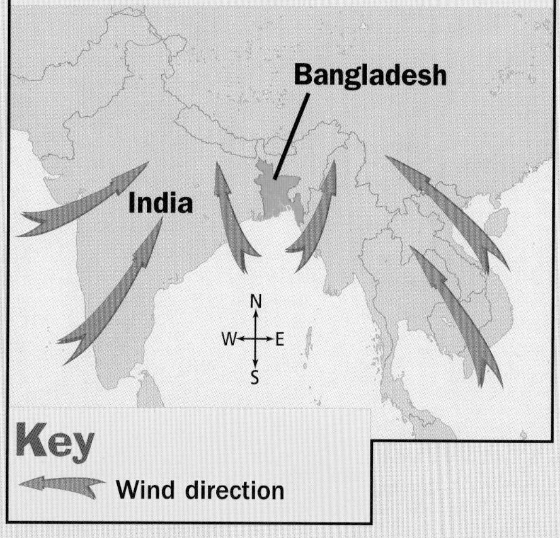

How the 1998 Flood Began

In the summer of 1998, the monsoon rains were very heavy in Bangladesh. It rained hard, and it rained for a long time. The snow melted as usual, and there were storms in the Bay of Bengal. The Ganges, the Meghna, and the Brahmaputra rivers all flooded at the same time.

The rivers started to rise in early July after very heavy rain at the end of June. They went over their banks and flooded two thirds of Bangladesh. Even the capital city of Dhaka was flooded.

The land stayed flooded until the last week in September.

Flooding in Dhaka, the capital city of Bangladesh

A woman wades through floodwater in search of drinking water during the flood.

The Effects of the Flood

The floods were disastrous for the people of Bangladesh. More than 1,000 people were killed. Many people died from diseases that spread in the floodwaters. People caught malaria, dysentery, and other serious diseases.

Other people were killed when they touched electrical power lines that were floating in the water. Poisonous snakes in the water were also a threat. Many people died from snakebites as they waded through the water.

Over half a million homes were destroyed by the flood. Crops were wiped out and animals were killed, so there was a shortage of food. The floodwaters polluted the fresh water, so drinking water was scarce.

Roads, railways, and bridges were also damaged. This made it very hard for rescuers to reach people in need. Many people could not be helped.

After the Flood

The **conclusion** summarizes the text.

It took Bangladesh a long time to recover after the flood. The damage was thought to have cost over 3 billion American dollars. Over 1,000 kilometers (621 miles) of roads and 100 bridges had been damaged or destroyed. People lacked food, shelter, and clean drinking water.

The flood had taken over most of the country. It had turned roads into rivers and swept away countless buildings and farms.

The Bangladesh flood was an example of how greatly changes in the weather can affect people's lives. It was a disaster the people of Bangladesh will never forget.

The 1998 flooding of Bangladesh affected the lives of millions of people.

Apply the Key Concepts

Key Concept 1 Conditions in the atmosphere, such as air pressure, create weather.

Activity

Make a list of the weather conditions that can lead to floods. When you have made your list, go to the library and get two more books on floods. Scan the books to find sections about weather conditions related to floods. Read these sections. Add to your list any new weather conditions you find.

Weather Conditions

1. monsoon rains
2.
3.

Key Concept 2 Clouds give meteorologists clues about what is happening in the atmosphere.

Activity

Draw a chart with three columns. In the first column, draw pictures of different kinds of clouds. In the second, name each kind of cloud and tell what it looks like. In the third, explain what each kind tells about the weather. Label your chart "Clouds and Weather."

Clouds and Weather

Key Concept 3 Tools and technology help meteorologists gather data about weather.

Activity

Conduct research to find more information about flood plains. Choose an area you know that floods regularly. Find out about the flood plain of this area, then write a description of the flood plain.

Flood Plain

RESEARCH AND WRITE

Create Your Own Explanation

There are lots of examples of extreme weather around the world. Some extreme weather may even happen close to where you live. Can you remember a flood or a drought? Can you remember a big storm that turned into a hurricane or caused a tornado?

1. Study the Model

Look back at the description of explanations on page 20. Then, read the article on pages 21–26 again. Look for the examples in the text that tell you this is an explanation. Can you find the opening statement? Can you find the concluding statement? Which paragraphs explain the causes of the weather disaster? Which paragraphs explain the effects of the weather disaster? Look at the diagrams or maps again. Think about how they helped you understand the topic.

2. Choose Your Topic

Now choose one example of an extreme weather event that you would like to find out more about. You may have to start by looking at books on extreme weather, reading newspaper accounts, or using the Internet. Once you've chosen your topic, you're ready to start.

3. Research Your Topic

Ask yourself what you already know about this topic. Do you know enough to write an explanation of how or why it occurred? Probably not. So, you need to make a list of questions that you need to answer. Remember that you are going to write an explanation, so many of your questions may start with "how" or "why." Now go to the library or to the Internet to get your facts.

Monsoon

1. What caused the monsoon?

2. How did the monsoon affect people?

4. Take Notes

Take notes of what you find out. As you find out a new fact, you may find that it leads to another question. Write the new questions down so that you don't forget them. As you write your notes, make a note of the things that you can explain using a diagram or map.

5. Write a Draft

Look back at the facts you found. Do they explain how or why your event occurred? If they do, start writing your draft. You may need to check back with page 20 to remind yourself of the features of an explanation.

6. Revise and Edit

Reread your draft. Does it explain your extreme weather event? Does it have all the features of an explanation? Have you spelled special weather words correctly? Have you drawn charts and maps to help with the explanation?

SHARING YOUR WORK

Present Your Explanation

Now you can share your work. With a group of students, present your explanations as part of a television special report on extreme weather. The program will be called *Explaining Extreme Weather*.

How to Present Your Work

1. **Choose a person in your group to be the anchorperson.**
   That person will introduce each member of the group. The anchorperson will also read the opening statement from each explanation.
2. **Collect the equipment you will need.**
   Before you make your presentation, you will need to transfer your charts and maps to overhead transparencies or to a piece of poster board.
3. **Rehearse your reading.**
   Before you read your explanation you will need to rehearse reading it aloud. Read it aloud several times. Practice looking up at your audience while you are speaking.
4. **When you have finished, be prepared to answer questions.**
   Your audience may ask you to explain something in more detail or review some of the facts.
5. **When you have all made your oral presentations, bind the explanations together and make them into a book.**
   As a group, make a cover for the book. Then, bind all the pages together with staples or yarn.

Glossary

air pressure – the effect of air pressing down on Earth's surface

atmosphere – the layer of air that surrounds Earth

data – information that is collected

flood plains – low-lying areas that flood after heavy rain

floods – the effect of too much water on the land, usually caused by a lot of rain

forecast – to predict what the weather will be like

front – a weather condition that occurs when areas of air with different temperatures meet

high air pressure – a weather condition that occurs when there is a lot of air pressing down on Earth

hurricanes – severe storms that start over warm seawater and bring strong winds, heavy rain, and huge waves

low air pressure – a weather condition that occurs when there is not much air pressing down on Earth

meteorologists – scientists who study the weather

satellites – objects that travel around Earth in space and send information back to Earth

vapor – small drops of water in the air that rise into the atmosphere

Index